A Record of Souls

By Steve Michaelis

Bonshi Go Publishing
Reno, Nevada

Copyright ©2021 Steve Michaelis

Bonshi Go Publishing

Reno, Nevada

All rights reserved. No part of this book may be reproduced or transmitted in any form, or by any means, electronic or mechanical, including photocopying, or by any information storage and retrieval system, without permission in writing from the publisher, except for the inclusion of brief quotation in a review.

Photography and book design by Robin P. Simonds, Beagle Bay Inc.

ISBN: 978-1-7346054-0-2

Library of Congress Control Number: 2021902087

First Edition

Printed in the United States of America

27 26 25 24 23 22 21   1 2 3 4 5 6 7 8 9 10

In the other life, whenever we think about someone, we call up that individual's face in our thought along with many details about her or his life; and when we do this, the other is called to us—Further, we talk with each other and continue to see each other in keeping with our friendship in the world. I have heard many people who had just come from the world overjoyed to see their friends again, and their friends overjoyed that they had arrived.

Emanuel Swedenborg
January 29, 1688 – March 29, 1772

Acknowledgements

I would like to thank Denise and Larry Barclay for early encouragement and for contributing to my understanding of what this is. And to Joseph Cacibauda for his preparation of the text and statements.

Of course, to my wife, Rieko Shimbo, who's support for this project in all its phases was essential. And to Nolan Cobin for his lessons in freedom, and to all of those who provided inspiration in the early development of this work.

This is dedicated to all of the souls who came forward to join in it.

A Record of Souls

Introduction

Somewhere in the All That There Is exists a record, an expanding, spiraling record of everyone that has ever been. The nature and form of this spiral is that of a coiled spring that has been formed into a circle. Picture a slinky toy that has been joined seamlessly at the ends and you will see it.

The circle has images of sentient souls in each loop within the spiral. Each image is a portrait with groups of symbols around it that gives information regarding that life that can be accessed in its entirety by anyone who can see it.

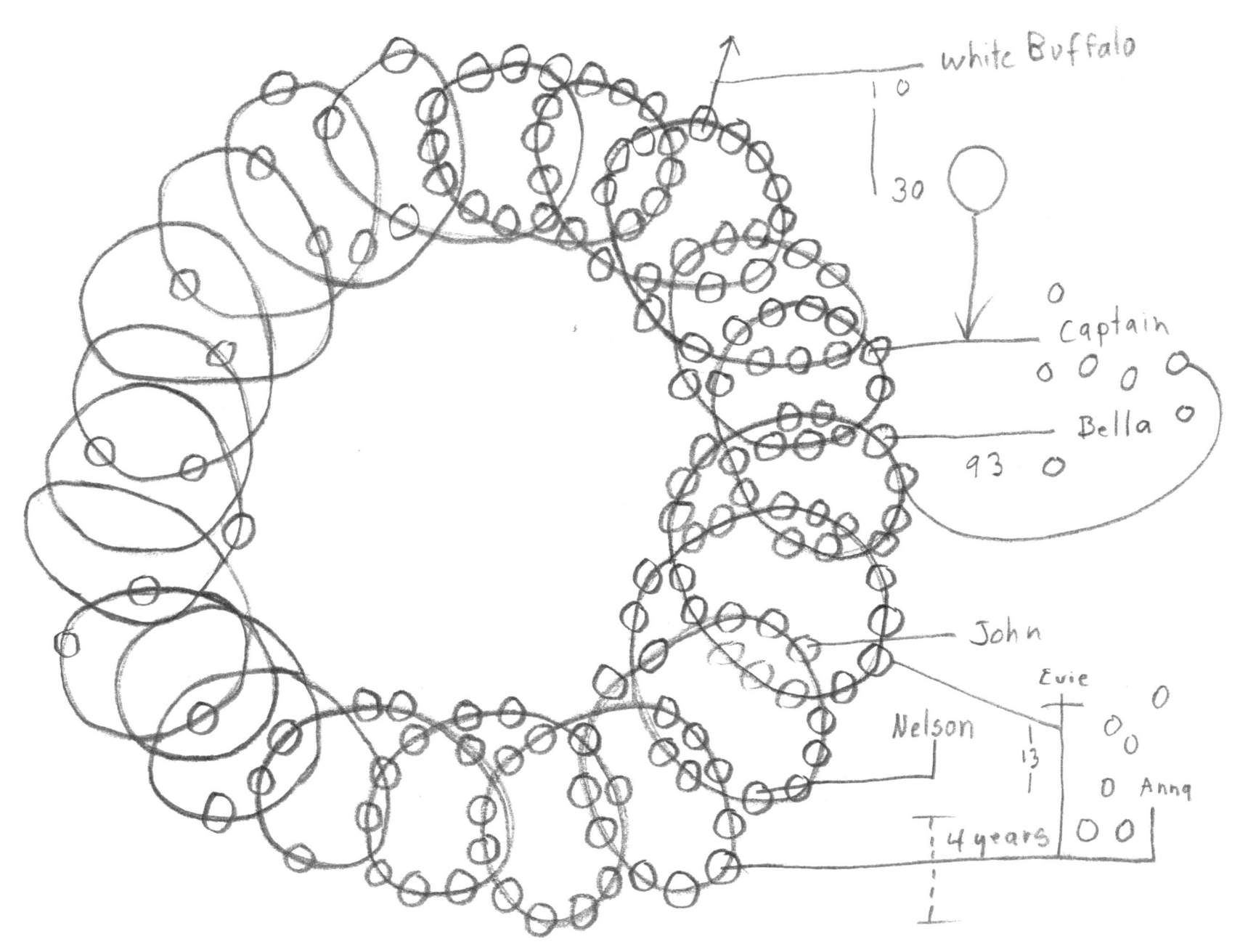

It is infinite and is ever-growing; expanding from within as more souls are added.

It is not sequential, however it is not random. It is organically growing yet mechanical in its function. It is a record of souls. Within that record, the details can be seen by everyone who has touched that life. Each image/symbol is a portal to the universe of that being as they are in the All That There Is, where and when they are.

When I was younger my art, dreams, and own experiences with coming close to crossing over led me to the ponderings that helped make me sensitive to people both here and in other realms. As a child, I remember drifting to sleep and seeing a stream of faces of people I had never seen before, that along with seeing written pages and reading them in that state. I didn't remember them because I didn't really understand it all. So I put them in the back of my consciousness until the day that I had the ability to see and understand that these people are trying to contact me and seek my help in getting the attention that they needed, the kind that they didn't get when they were in the world.

My contribution was that I had develop the skills as an artist, skills as a reader of their stories and the sensitivity to feel what it is that they wanted to say.

I am 66 years old as I write this. It's taken me this long to be ready and able to take on a project like this, through art, meditation, spirit travel practices, and the experiences of the mystical too numerous to convey.

The artwork in this book was done on the paper sleeves that held 78 RPM records from long ago. I found a whole book of them and dismantled the bindings, making them ready to draw on. But the paper of the record sleeves was fragile, so great care had to be taken.

As I became acquainted with the people and beings I was called upon to chronicle, I was informed as to what medium to use: colored pencils, pastel or paint. It came to me that the sleeves are the appropriate place to put the

portraits. I came to know the people better by spending the time as it was needed to satisfy their wanting to be portrayed in this work. I did it as simply but as thoroughly as I could. The portraits are surrounded by the field of the sleeves that held all of the elements that gave a definition as to what they did with themselves when they were here. I was happy to have been of service to their need to be represented at this level.

The depiction is vastly simplified by necessity in order to bring it into view.

Motion for All

My work was always my first love.
It's all I wanted to do.
The machines and the tools of my trade were my
freedom.
With my dog as my best helper, we got greasy and dirty
as we made the world of motion,
spinning and traveling, for people in the city of wonders.
I can work on this fantastic machinery
forever.

Quiet and Cold

My power came from the confluence of Heaven and Earth.
I lived in and saw both clearly.
My power enabled me to answer questions.
Many people came to my door and I helped them;
and, there was an exchange.
Under the cold white blanket, the Earth and its features were masked and
sleeping quietly.
I could see clearly against the bright backdrop the answers
I and they were seeking given silently.
As silently as the snow.

The Sound of Magic

My teacher made it known that someday the tools and instruments of my
magic could be lost or taken away.
But, while we had them,
we created the very powerful sound of magic for and from
the Mother of Creation.
When those things—tools, instruments, rituals, were taken from us, the
memory of them was so strong that all we
needed to do was close our eyes and see within.
Hear the sounds of the good work we did.
We knew that the threads of our work were reaching forward to a day
when all would be returned to our descendants.

The Provider

While I was in form with a body,
everything we needed was there.
It was plentiful and beautiful.
It was a part of us to use, gather, and hunt.
We created ourselves from where we were,
and we knew that it was the truth

A Beautiful Friendship

She was properly cared for and loved; and, she shared with me her product.
We were friends in our business together.
I never wanted more out of it than she received.
Our simple lives became great joy.
My objects were the symbols, reminders of my work and my life of love.
She came to me as a baby and I had to learn and know closely what she did with her life and what I could do with
what she gave.
She was the giver of milk that I could refine into the products that people need.
We were a helpful team, each and all members of my family.

The Proof

From my hidden place, I affected one who sensed I was there.
The picture in front of me, my cover was complete and attractive to the child.
I lingered for decades in my comfortable place until in a random act of maintenance, I was revealed to the child,
now a man; and, the attraction was explained.
Trust how you feel. There is something inside of it.
The cause of your dreamlike wonderment was not what you thought. It was me all along.
Your guide to the proof of things unseen.

Through Thought

In the most orderly way I could manage, my thoughts became my world
and life.
Through reason, my influences guided me to be productive.
My occupations were created to meet the needs of others.
I was happy to be able to see the beauty of the results
through thought.

through thought

27

Captain John

Until I found my land, I didn't feel love for anything.
I became connected to it and I felt responsible for it.
I was committed to taking care of it the way I did my family, so that there was always room to grow, a place to expand.
When I worked the land, my mind was free from all the terrible things I saw in that war.
I loved my land and the tools I used to derive my family's living.
I had never known anything as satisfying, peaceful, and quiet. So quiet.

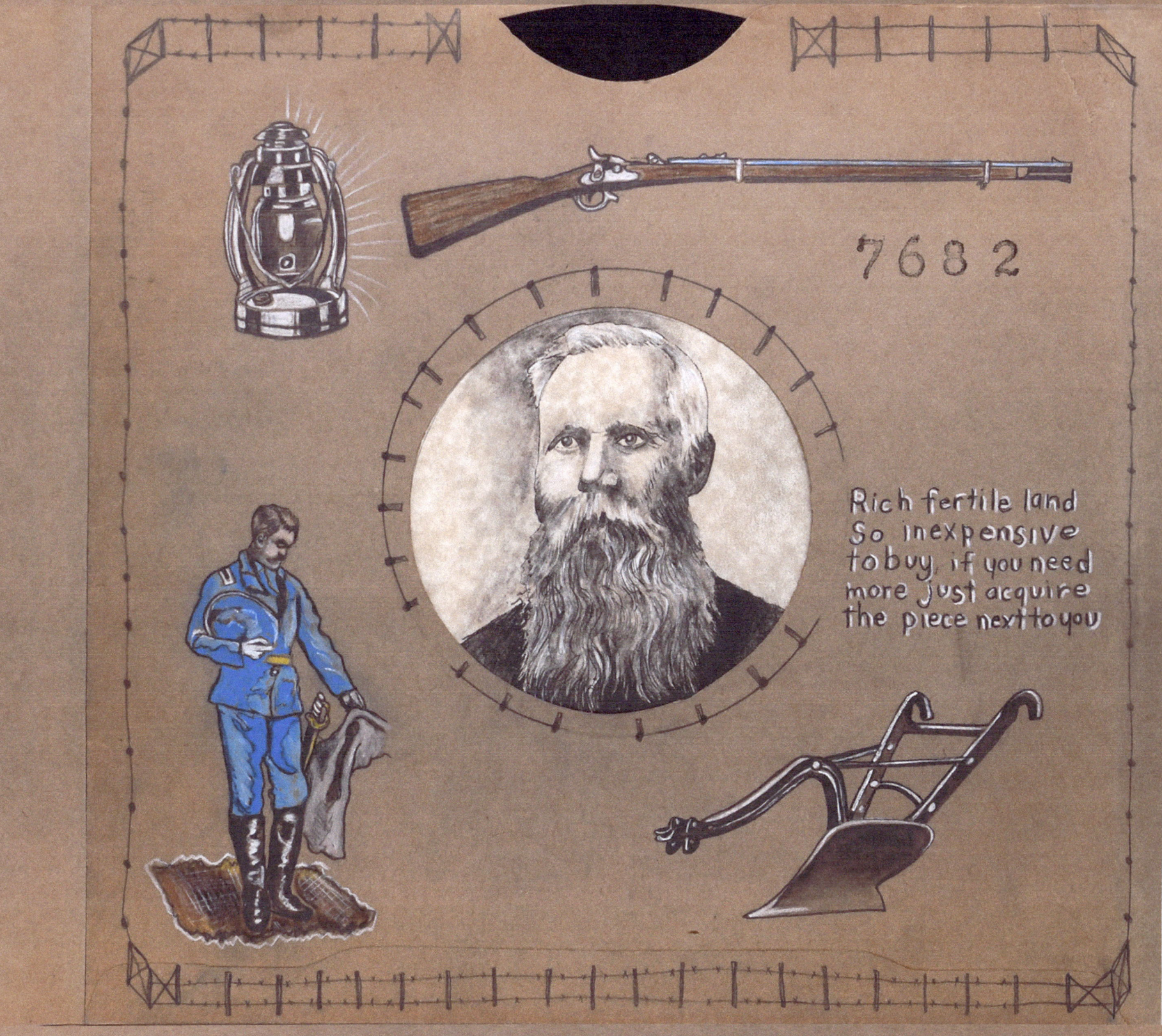

Helper

I am one form of the guardian that is helpful.
I can protect and guide you to the good in what you seek.
I can guide you and block you from that which is harmful or not useful.
In one form or another I protect, steer, and take care of you on your journey.

The Unformed

I'm not a ghost. I was incomplete. I came that way.
I was able to see what I did and that was as much as I could do.
In the beginning, I did not know very much nor could I see how they did.
I'm here now and able; but, not then.
I was taken care of by the other ones Baa, Nom, Enn, Knu, and Noom.
I didn't know what I was; but, I'm beginning to know now.
Unlike before, I can speak now and learn.

Ventriloquist

The Invisible Voice from Within
It is not from me, but it comes through me
as the person's spirit, flowing through, creating the voice and the
personality that is manifested in the moving-doll creation.
Through their wishing and my assistance, they appear before us to be
seen and heard.
It is a form of birth that is able to live by my hand.

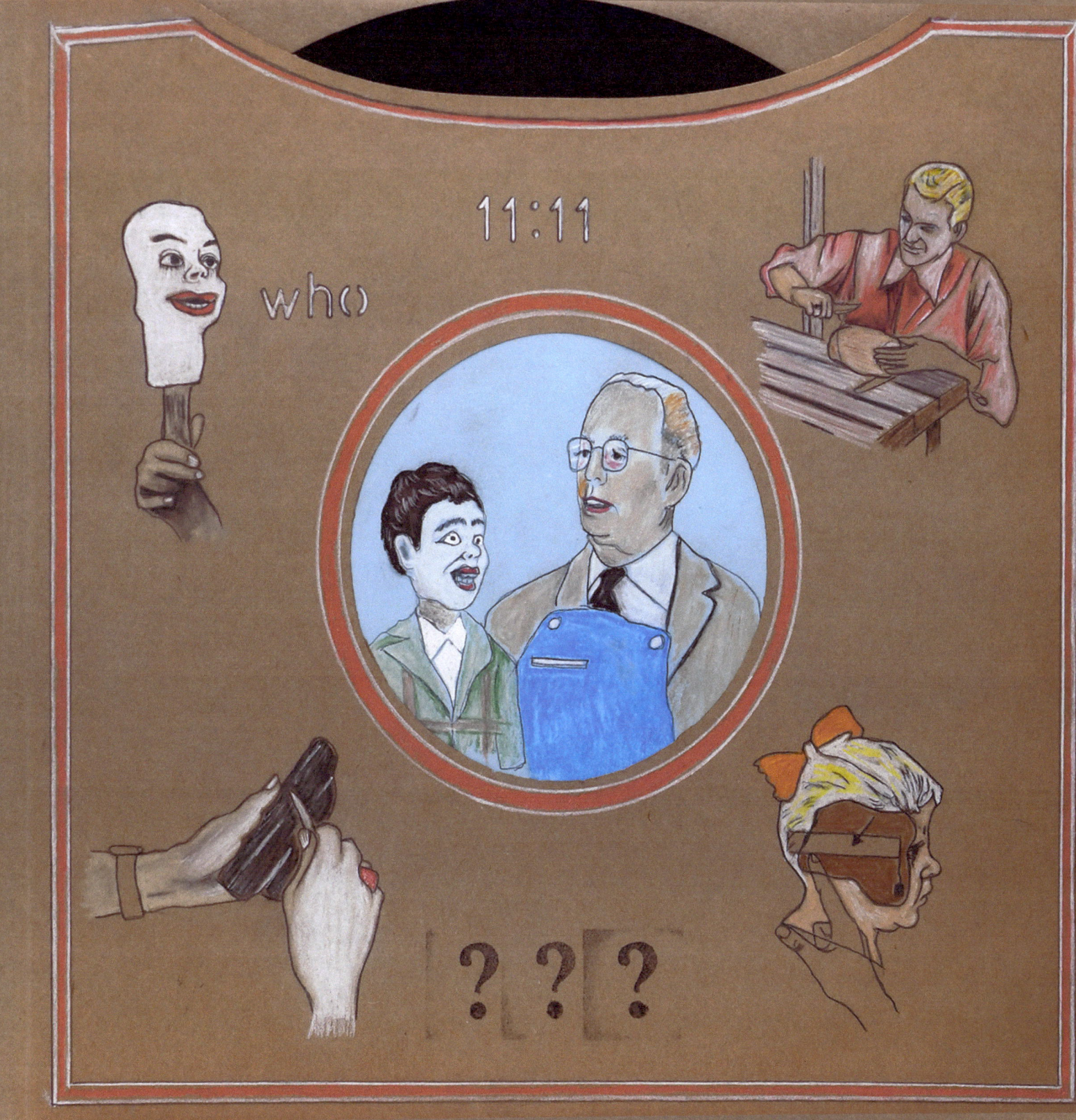

The Deep Forest

Alone with my weapons to gather and kill.
In the daytime, with the sun above and the leaves creating a darkness.
I enter the deep forest. I'm afraid and exited about getting the most important thing—food for my people.
My ancestors gave me the tools and vision to see, hear, and smell, and to be strong so that I always return home with
what is needed.
I live for them because we are all one.

Sea Captain

My life, my inner and outer, were one thing. The sea and everything that went along with it in my time. I could barely think about anything else unless it was related to and supported that one thing. From the very beginning of my thoughts and through a long life to the eventual end. One life, one thought, longing, one love. I was fortunate to have such a love to guide me and give me so much in a successful and complete life that filled every moment with what I wanted from the start.

John

The experience of my childhood was elusive and crowded out with the limitations of survival. I labored my whole life, from the time I could work until I left the world. It was good for that time and place, it was normal, and I fit in it comfortably. I was strong. I didn't see what a child having fun was until I peered through the gate and saw the colors and toys and laughter and fun, and I was able to go there and become complete.

Mr. Nelson

There's nothing like a fresh bright coat of paint.
You feel happy when you step back and look at the thin veneer, and know it uplifts the surrounding areas in a
cheerful way.
That's why I painted these buildings, to add color and brightness to all of our lives.
To give to my community-not just bright paint, but brightened spirits.

The Little Seamstress (Hope)

From here where I am now, I can see what happened to me in my life. I was given away at birth, or perhaps thrown away having no value just a thing to be gotten rid of. I lived my childhood with others like me, in a large dark building. I was given what I needed to stay alive. As I grew, I learned how to fix clothing and things made of cloth. The cloth was quiet. Quiet was good. I fixed others' clothing always with hopes of having some value and usefulness; but I never found it. The others didn't see me. It was as if I wasn't even there and I didn't matter.

In that time, one who had no value wasn't able to live a long life; but, looking back from here, from this other place, I can see that at least it seems that I did matter after all.

Photographer

The outer eye. The inner eye.
I brought these images from the world into me with the aid of a mechanical device.
I learned where they come from.
The outer is the inner.
My body's eye is the eye of my mind;
and the camera is the tool that joins them.

The Eternal Gallery

Please come with us. We'll show you around and explain everything. We know everything about this place. This is the infinite eternal gallery where every work of art, everything that has been done or will be done anywhere is kept; even ideas that weren't actually finished are here. We take care of them too so you can see them. Even though our place is as large as the universe, you can easily get around. We can take you where your tendencies want to go. If you get tired and want to stop, just go through any doorway and you will be back at the beginning, here with us.

Always remember that everywhere in the space of the gallery, forever takes a moment, and every grain of sand has a name.

Bubble Man

One simple thing I loved my entire life was to capture air inside these floating spheres.
The colors, the gentle drifting, and spinning on an invisible axis all calmed and fascinated my child-like mind.
To make it greater, so I might share the joy with others, I needed to accomplish smaller things: that served the greater, to form my company, earn a living.
How could it be that I never understood why I wanted nothing else?
One simple thing.
So happy.

The Good Wife

I always loved to reach out and talk to the folks in my township in the country, to plan activities for service, celebrations, births, deaths, weddings, anything that celebrates my involvement. I liked to be in the middle of activities involving my friends and neighbors. I need to be a part of things in my community, my church, and my people. One can always create something, with help that is good and helpful to others. That's what made my life complete and happy. The country, the states, the counties, the townships, the properties, the people, all for me to be in.

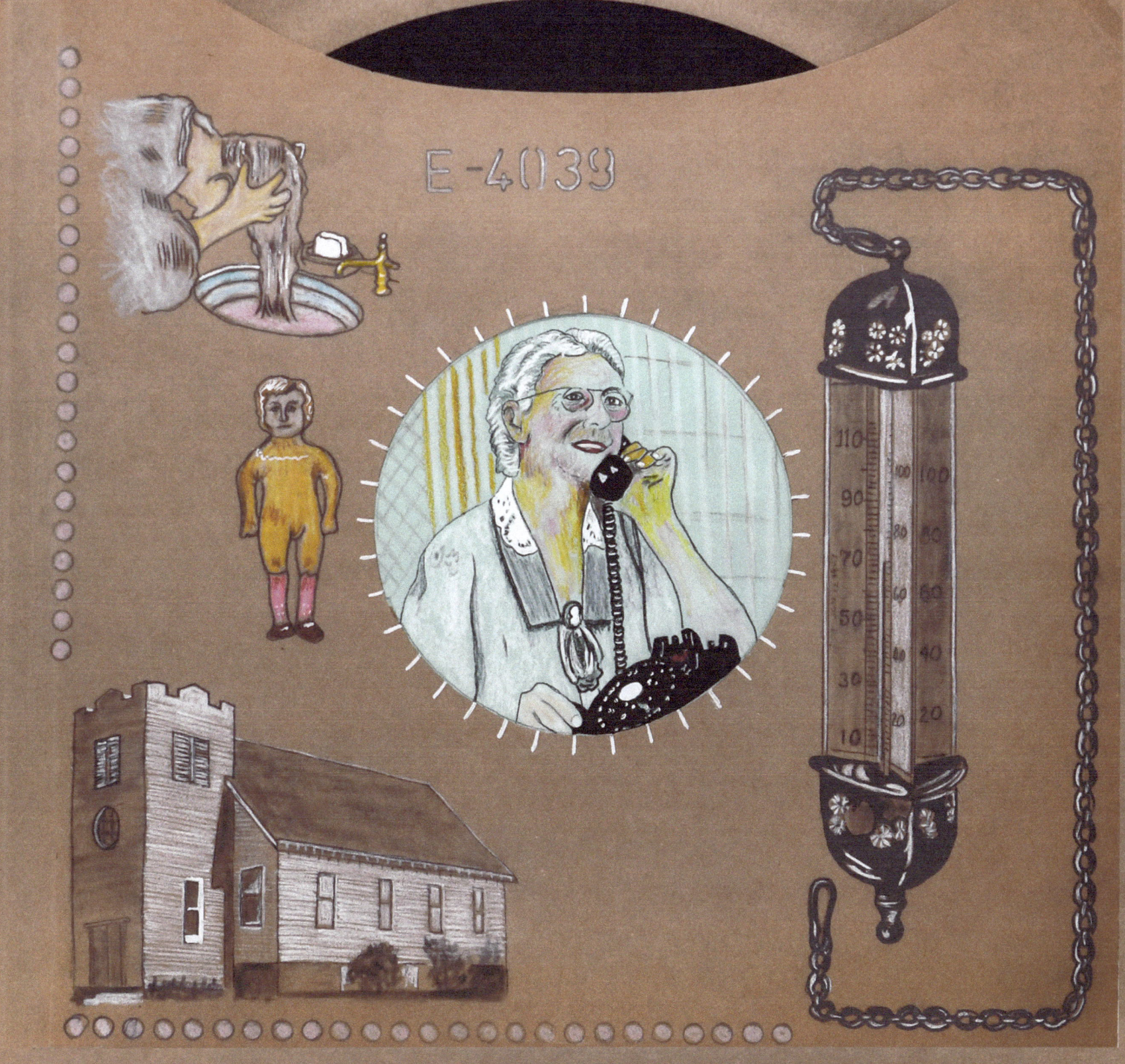

The Pretty One

I know now that I used the adornments to my perceived personal beauty
to enhance the possibility of acceptance, But, I never seemed to find it.
In all my shopping and dressing up, I kept searching in that small place
in my soul.
I lived with a kind of love that put me on a pedestal.
It was good for a while, but nothing lasts.
The happiness I found in that shallow world went away and
I again was alone, even while surrounded by others.
I know that it was something I needed to go through to find the larger
Me.
But, I didn't like the pain then, and I still don't

Briefly a Bride

Everything was so beautiful. He was. I was. Life was.
We planned to live out our happiness.
We loved our life together; but the happiness was brief.
The shock of the loss sent me into a void I never came out of.
The sadness lives in me with an overwhelming power.
So much love, life, happiness taken from me so suddenly was more than
I could carry.
I could not be helped.
Even the passage of time could not rescue me.

The Country Doctor

The 19th century magical powers of doctor-hood in the small community are a part of my work. The objects I use for healing have a life of their own and they need as much credit for existing as I, myself, do .

I'm somewhere in between a healer and a modern doctor. I can treat and cure illness by seeing the treatment in my mind's pictures and by applying the remedy using more modern tools.

All the senses need to be used: sight smell, sound, taste; and, maybe most importantly, how I feel about the problem. Once I have gathered all the information I can about the person and the malady, I then begin the work of curing and fixing the physical ailment based on the unique combinations that make up the structure of each individual patient.

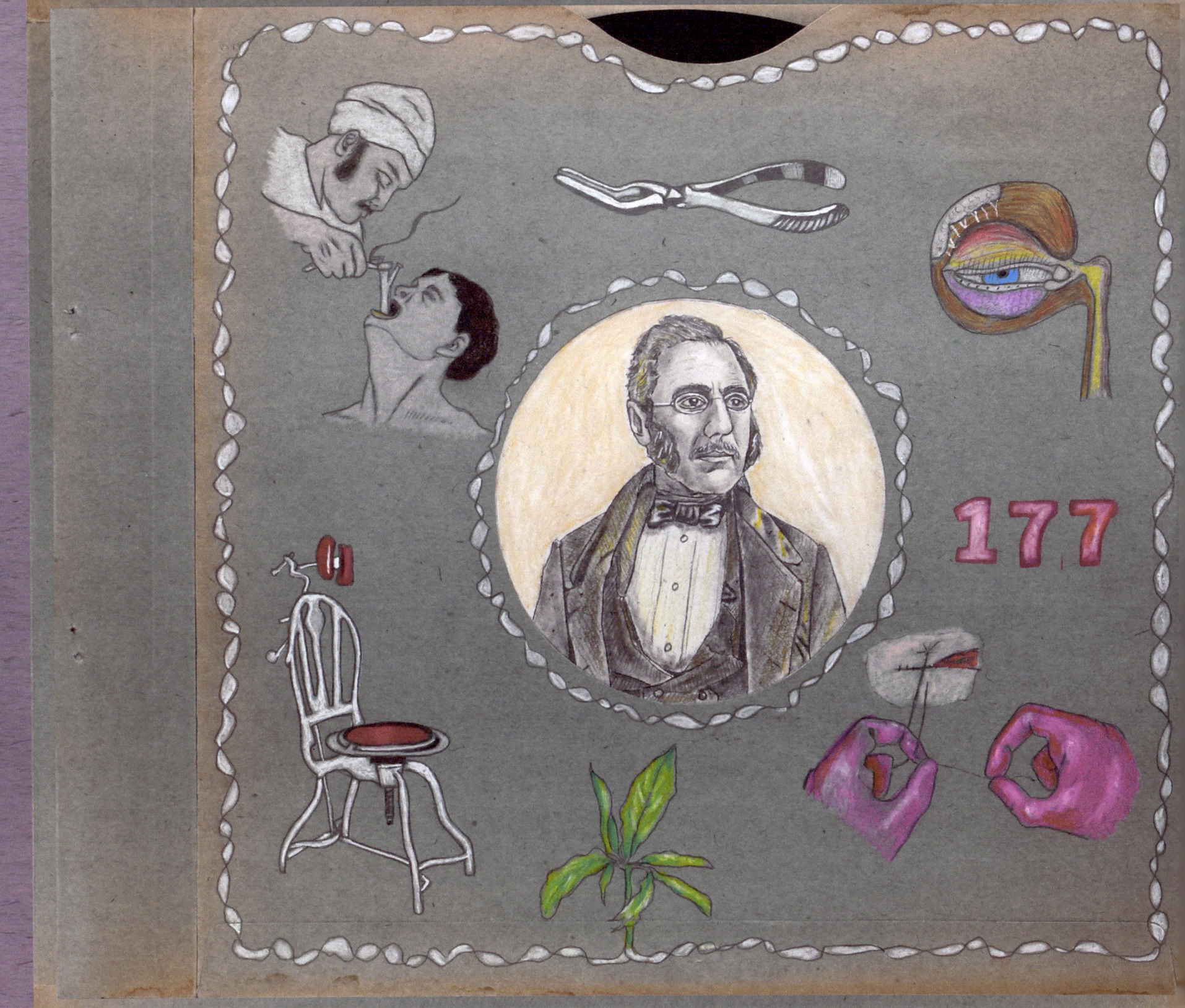

Twins for Me

The beautiful blessings of my life. My twin baby girls. I never expected to have such a gift. The many acts of wonderment that I lived, the teaching of them and the guiding their lives to do good work. The farm was a good classroom for learning to love the work. The rewards were clear and meaningful every day. Good chores led to a good life, and to the happiness in watching the growth. Everything was times two and the closer I looked, every day I could see how different they were inside. More different than they looked. They grew and grew. They were my miracles and each day was filled with them. What more can a miracle be?

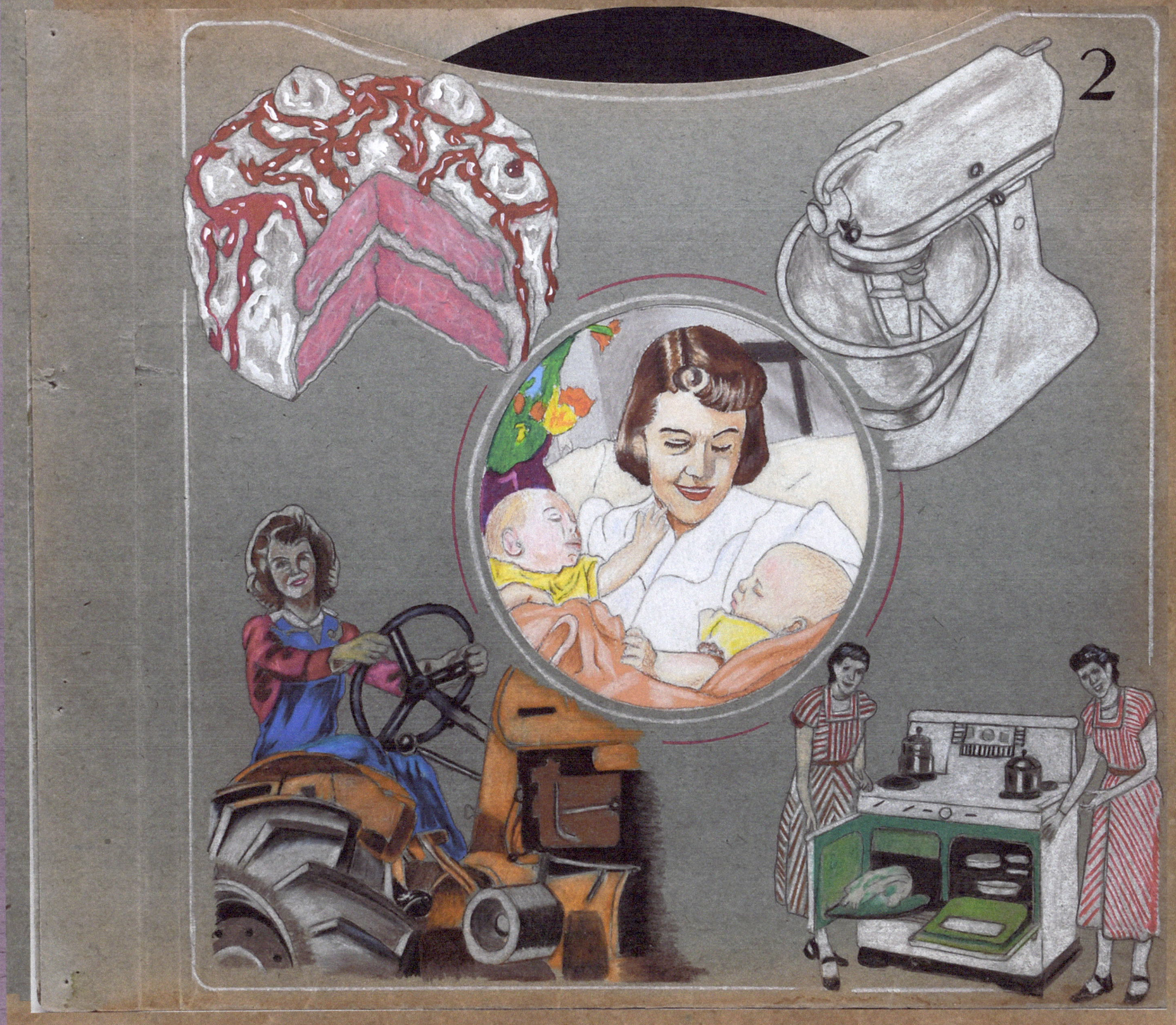

Lovely Dreamer

The façade dissolves in my dreams.
Whatever troubled the pretty young lady now becomes a picture.
I lived a tired life where the inner didn't match the outer.
I felt it in an extreme way, but I always kept it to myself,
never revealing the things I saw at night.
At night, the dreams went on and on, and in the morning,
there was the make-up, the hair, the painted smile
to give the falsities that I needed to live.
I could never find the balance. What could I have done to find it?

Old Joe

The peaceful changing of one thing, place, and time, to another, the events and moments of his life seemed to stack up like receipts on a spindle. He spent the later years reviewing the spindle's contents. Although he seemed to be doing nothing. It could be that it was the busiest time ever for him. The memories and their availability to him were a function of his life that could not be overlooked. In his silence and stillness, each event of his life wafted him otherward on the drift of his rising as he went upstairs.

OLD JOE

went upstairs

Kitchen Lady

How to Make Bread:
Scald four cups of milk
Add ½ cup of sugar
3 teaspoons salt
6 tablespoons shortening
Cool to lukewarm
Dissolve yeast in ½ cup warm water
Add 3½ cups warm water and yeast to milk mixture
Sift and measure 6 quarts of flour.
Mix well with hands.
Let stand in warm place for 2 to 4 hours.
Knead and allow to rise 1 to 2 hours.
Bake 1 hour in at 350 degrees Fahrenheit in a greased loaf pan.

Lady Mechanic

I couldn't believe something as crazy as a war could bring about something helpful to me in my life; but my career fixing cars and trucks came about because all the men were off fighting. It turns out I was good at it; good enough that the town's people noticed me. I was surprised that I had the skill to do the job and to eventually have my own shop. I made a good living and had a good life as a mechanic; and, most of all, I enjoyed it. I was more useful in this than I think I could have been doing anything else. It was just meant for me.

Music from Heaven

As the notes floated upward
they carried my message to the divine cause.
Creating the music,
I knew that passing on the ways of making it
was all I needed to do.
It was a complete thing.
Guidance came on wings of joy
telling me what I could, and
I must do.
No other love could be so great.
So complete.

Indentured

I spent my early life in servitude for a debt my parents incurred.
For eleven years I worked to pay for something I would never receive.
Without reward, my goal was to be free and make my own way in life.
My anger became my motivation,
and through time, also became my guiding star.

Never Enough

Looking at it from where I am now it seems as if all the bad things, all the wrong things that I did, I did not because I enjoyed being like that, but because I felt the need to cover up my actions, my character, my thoughts, and feelings. They all had to be concealed from others. In cultivating these wrongs, I was insuring that I had something to hide and that was all I cared about. Being sneaky was the main purpose of all of my crimes. They all stem from that and it was so throughout my life until its unnatural end.

Hunter

Simply searching, I feel that's what I did. Roaming the land with simple tools that I carried with me at all times. Searching, ready to bring in to the table food from the land. Everything, all of it came from there and I built myself around what was there for me to live on. My food, but also my life, the joy of the air, the beauty of the running and flight were simple ways to merge together with life and death, happiness and sadness, it and me.

Convalescent

Having an illness which takes you away from your child requires all of the strength you can find in your mind and in your soul. I was so far away and I couldn't even tell them what I was doing. I was alone no matter where I was or who I was with. Without my family I was alone. So I waited for my body and my legs to heal, which required a strong mind. I kept strong by seeing every day the images of my life, my boy, my man, my home, and everything in it until I was complete again and was able to go back to them. The greatest sign that I was well again was our baby daughter born a year after I got home.

Shining Armor

I wore my armor because it not only protected me, but also limited me by its hardness. It became so much a part of my body that I felt strange without it.

I was trained to have a sense of duty and honor and I enforced my duties with love, religion, and war. This life gave me freedom and honor; yet, I stood ready to give it all up at a moment's notice for my queen without question. My love for those above me, and my disdain for those below me gave me my place.

Religious Artist

My religion was my art
and I sought to follow the given instructions
from the source of all information.
I worked alone, always alone.
I was chosen to put the thoughts and feelings that came to me
into the forms.
I had no choice.
We all had our special tasks in those times.
Only we could do them.
I believed in that then.

Fighter Pilot

When I flew above everything,
I now wonder
Was that pursuit what I thought it was for the world then?
I was so far removed from what I was causing below
yet now, I can't get away from it.
What do I owe?
What do I pay?
How do I pay?
I can't move now.
I'm just here writing to find a way out.
Once I moved so freely,
so quickly.
I now see that
My service in flight was for the wrong reasons.

The Good Cop

Being in the military taught me how to be in service to others. That is how I saw my profession: taking care of the people in my neighborhood, on my watch, and on my beat. At night as I walked alone, my uniform, its color and shape, separated and protected me. I wanted to protect; and in my profession it was the best way for me to protect my small area of the world.

Tools of Life

I'm speaking now from a different voice than I had before.
Before, survival was my only concern.
My basic, elegant tools were simply made, designed to
quickly get food for my tribe.
I was the hunter and supplier for our lives.
One life sacrificed itself to become another life.
No regrets, no glory, just an exchange.
All that was necessary, that I saw for life.

A Traveler

In traveling to faraway lands, I found people everywhere willing to trade. I was able to travel all over the world with no interference because I was a man of trade. I brought valuable items back to my homeland, things the people had never seen, but could own. I lived a life of wonderment of the faraway land, how their people differed in all of the products they created. In my time, I was only really interested in seeing and experiencing all that I could of everything in the world.

Free

I feel very much in place where I am now with all the possibilities for me. I wasn't really in the world when I was there. I was there but I wasn't there as I am here, but not here. I am in the here and there both at once and that is how it is. Earth-bound prison in one moment. Flying free to instantly be anywhere in the next. Violent highs and lows that stretch you almost to breaking with the purpose of expansion into the freedom of the all that there is.

The Contender

There I was dropped into the middle of a desperate life with no skills. All I had was rage, but with training I learned to vent my rage only in the ring with other desperate fighters. I guess it's true that after so many poundings, you can have the rage knocked out of you and so I did. It wasn't easy to find something else to do, but I had it in me. I just didn't know it or see it. But I found a little of piece of it in me and with the other feelings that were left when the rage went away I worked on the skills I had for business, It grew and I found a new life that was more peaceful, useful, and successful.

Old Wood

These tools allow me to get into the heart of the old wood I used; at first invisible, then shown to be a thin veneer of age. It works the same with people. But the tools, ah, the tools were more important than they looked at first. These things I worked with to me were more important than I was. I neglected most of my life much to my regret. I did work that didn't require any of the courage that it takes for other things in life, wife, family, friends, or knowledge, just me and the things I made from old wood and the fresh new wood inside.

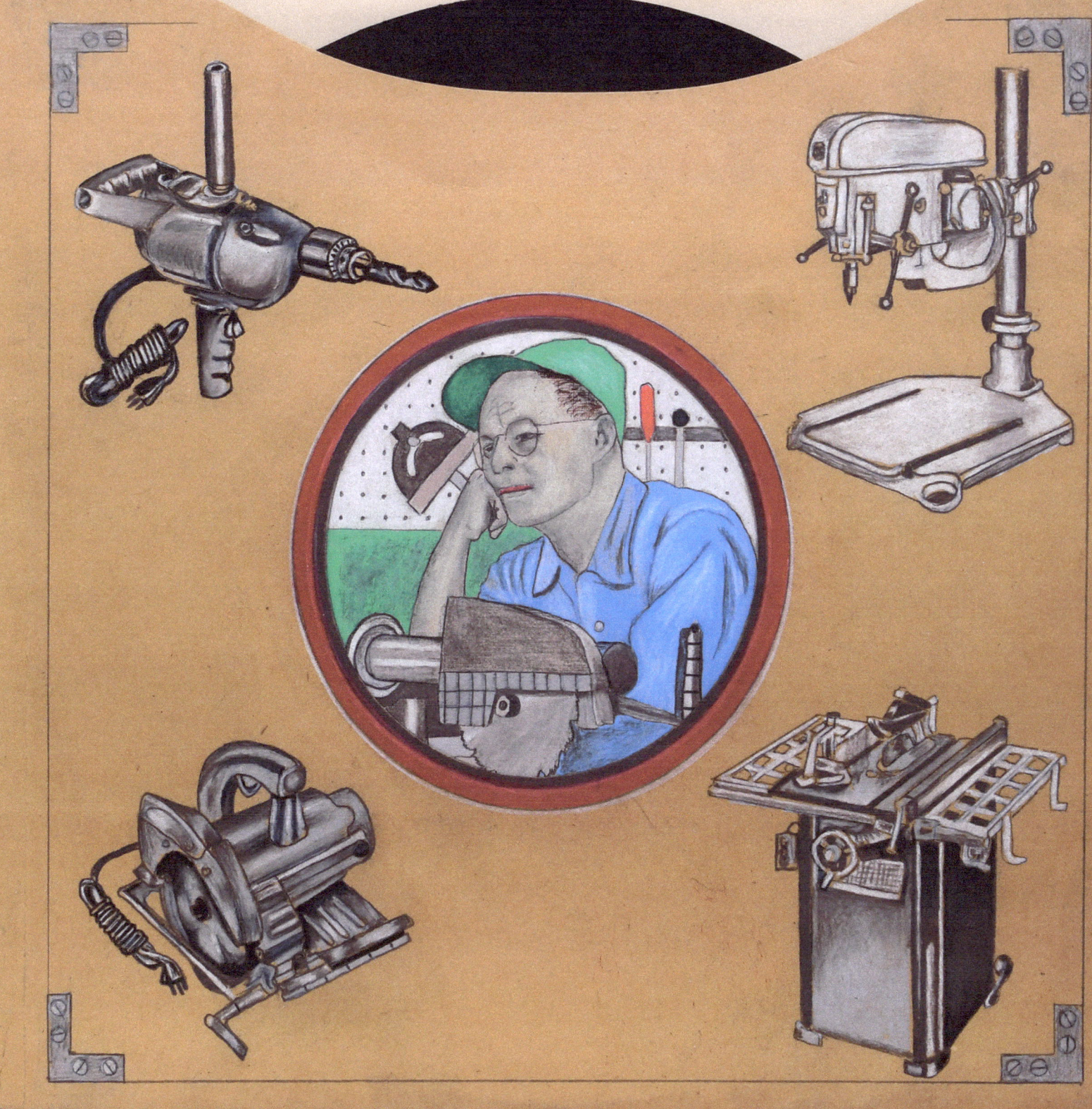

The Player

All that I can say about the game is that I felt really alive when I was on the field. It was more important to me than anything else. I was lucky to play and make a modest living from it. When you love an activity that much, you're naturally pretty good at it. I think I was somewhere between good and sort of average; but, I loved it and never seriously did anything else.

Bella

I came here as a little girl not knowing where I was after the big water where so many were lost and thrown over into the water. They still come to me and talk to me when I sleep, but I'm not afraid. I remember the big water and my life here more than where I came from. And even when life is mean I can still see some beauty around me, sometimes. And yet I understand that I'm being treated badly even though I've never known anything else.

Beautiful Silk

A bird, a song, a butterfly, and flower,
things of beauty to have around me.
To me they are as food, air, and water: necessary.
My desire was to be like them
delicate, graceful, and loving.
My body was smooth and soft like the silk I wore.
Both body and silk came from other beings who
gave their bodies to make them possible.
Beauty was my teacher.
Silk threads, like those of my life, reached forward
to a time when I could be returned.

Her Astronomy

I had reached as far as I could at the time given the primitive tools that I had. A young girl didn't fit into such a field or occupation as that. I just had to remember each day that with curiosity and courage I could do good things. Knowing that science was certainly a big part of the picture, but not all of it, I continued without being overwhelmed, especially when I got to a certain point in studying the universe and infinity where the numbers became so large that I, a human, couldn't use them anymore. My astronomy now required a different mindset and state of being to find a personal solution.

Home Servant

My employment as a servant made it possible for me to live a useful and happy life. The family I worked for was kind and thoughtful. They respected all people, seeing them worthy of consideration. I felt lucky to be connected to my fellow workers and my family, and to have the tools and objects to make my work fruitful. I never had the difficulties other servants had with other families. I worked with joyful energy to always be helpful to all in this home, which I felt was my home, too.

The Hovering Mother

The severity that I had in my mind and soul I think was brought on by the stories of tragedy I had heard and the ones I experienced myself. I couldn't stop imagining terrible things. I worried all the time and took all of the possible steps to prevent anything from taking place that could be harmful to my loved ones. I was left with all the work to maintain my house and son and the farm when my husband died. Every day, all day, the work, the vigilance, the diligence that it took to maintain my life. As a widow and mother it was difficult to stay strong. My looking-forward-hope is in my son taking it all over when he can.

My New Home

The ship went down with me in it. I recall I was bound for a new life in a new land but I never arrived. The storm was violent above the waves but it was calm and peaceful below them as I sank lower into the depths of the sea and gradually gave up the dream of my life for a dream of the next. I carried with me the pictures of the silent deep as my body drifted down and my soul drifted up in a beautiful separation.

A Charming Child

My mommy and daddy took such good care of me and gave me everything I wanted; then one day, everything changed. Suddenly, I was in a new place where everything was very pretty and nice. I didn't know where I was and I guess I still don't know this place.

One day a man asked me if I wanted to be in a picture book. I didn't understand so he showed me some other people who were in it already and it seemed nice so I said that it would be all right.

It has helped me to know more and see more. I'm glad I went in the book now I can see better where I was, where I am, and where I'm going.

www.ingramcontent.com/pod-product-compliance
Lightning Source LLC
Chambersburg PA
CBHW041818080526

44587CB00004B/134